D1561719

ABANDONED EASTERN PENNSYLVANIA

BEHIND THE BOARDS

KARI MILLER

AMERICA
THROUGH TIME®
ADDING COLOR TO AMERICAN HISTORY

America Through Time is an imprint of Fonthill Media LLC
www.through-time.com
office@through-time.com

Published by Arcadia Publishing by arrangement with Fonthill Media LLC
For all general information, please contact Arcadia Publishing:
Telephone: 843-853-2070
Fax: 843-853-0044
E-mail: sales@arcadiapublishing.com
For customer service and orders:
Toll-Free 1-888-313-2665

www.arcadiapublishing.com

First published 2022

Copyright © Kari Miller 2022

ISBN 978-1-63499-390-6

Typeset in Trade Gothic 10pt on 15pt
Printed and bound in England

CONTENTS

PREFACE

I have always had a healthy curiosity when it comes to abandoned and derelict places. Sometimes, these places remain untouched and almost frozen in time. Other times, they are empty, leaving nothing but the mystery of who once occupied the structure and why they left. That is the question I ask myself most often: Why is this place abandoned?

I am not entirely sure what attracts me to abandoned spaces so intensely, but I do know where it all started. I grew up in a small town in New Jersey. The kind of small town that had one post office for the whole town and where everyone had a P.O. box. So small, even, that all the grades from kindergarten to 12th shared the same bus.

Around the corner from my house sat an abandoned school. One night, my mom and my stepdad thought they would scare us by driving around the half-circle drive in front of the school while telling us a terrifying story of the headmaster of the school. As they recounted to us, the headmaster used to beat the children, which led to the school's shutting down. To this day, I am not sure if that story is true or not.

It was not long after that night that my stepbrother, Scott, and I snuck down to the school. We rode our bikes so we could get away quickly if needed. We snuck around the back of the school and dropped our bikes in the grass. The school's playground was still there but was overgrown with foliage. I still remember the descent down the staircase to the school's basement. We did not have flashlights or any idea of what we were doing. I was only in second grade at the time, though being in grade school might have been why I had this infatuation with the abandoned school.

We made our way to the first floor. I will never forget the smell. Those of you who have never ventured inside an abandoned place, it is hard to explain the smell of it, but I will try. It is a smell you can practically taste—of stale air, of rot. The lack of air circulation and the water damage create a unique aroma—an aroma that gets even worse if there is furniture and carpeting left behind.

I wish I could say I remember the place in explicit detail, but I was so young. I remember cobwebs, creaky floors, dust, and, of course, the smell. I remember being terrified and excited all at once. We came upon a room that had desks lined up in rows, the way most traditional classrooms are set up. There were books on the desks, making it seem as if the students could return at any time. The empty classrooms, untouched and undisturbed for years, fascinated me. I cannot tell you how many times my stepbrother and I snuck back into the school, but I just remember it was a weekly occurrence.

I moved away a few years later and said goodbye to my dilapidated playground. But I did not say goodbye to my curiosity. In high school, I took over five photography classes. Something about capturing moments, people, and places was incredible to me. I had the ability to freeze time, to create a permanent memory. It was not long before I was taking photos of everything.

A few years after graduating high school, I returned to my hometown to find that the school had become an empty field. And I did not have a single photograph of it. Which leads me to why I take photos of abandoned locations. Why, for me, exploring abandoned places is more than just a hobby or an adventure. These places are pieces of history that I can preserve in photographs. People today—and generations after—will know that these homes, buildings, and places once existed.

ABOUT THE AUTHOR

KARI MILLER has been a competent photographer for over eight years. She began exploring abandoned locations during elementary school. She grew up in a very small town and would often sneak into the town's abandoned school. Since a young age, her desire to explore abandoned locations has only grown. In high school, she was introduced to photography and learned both film and digital photography. She then began photographing abandoned locations while she explored them. Kari has traveled all over the East Coast and the Midwest regions of the United States exploring an abundance of locations. Kari loves taking pictures, collecting history, and observing what people have left behind.

INTRODUCTION

Pennsylvania was once the heartland of steel production and coal mining. By the mid-1990s, the coal industry in Eastern Pennsylvania died, leaving industrial workers in a postindustrial economy.

Philadelphia was once referred to as the "workshop of the world." After World War II, competition emerged, devastating the heavily reliant manufacturing cities in Eastern Pennsylvania. Changes in technology led to streamlined processes and limited the need for workers. Many lost their jobs due to plant closings and down-sizing. Hospitals closed due to outpatient treatment availability. Schools shut down as populations decreased. Churches lay in ruins as fewer people attended services. Today, many of these structures remain, vacant and unused.

1

ALLENTOWN STATE HOSPITAL

Allentown State Hospital (ASH) was established in 1901, but it was not until October of 1912 that the hospital opened. At the time, the facility was known as the Pennsylvania State Homeopathic Asylum for the Insane. Located on a bank near the Lehigh River between Allentown and Bethlehem, the institution was built to house 1,000 patients. The hospital was designed by Philip H. Johnson and was built in a block plan with corridors that connected the buildings. Among the buildings were two chapels, four patient wards, an operating room, an administration building, a kitchen, a dining room, an ice plant, a laundry facility, a boiler house, and an electric plant. Within a year of the hospital's opening, it was almost at full capacity, due to overcrowded nearby hospitals transferring patients to the facility.

Allentown State Hospital accepted patients mostly from a five-county service area. To avoid overcrowding, additional buildings were added to the property. Over two decades, staff housing, additional wards, a reception building for new admissions, and many others were added. In 1930, the hospital opened a children's ward—the first of its kind. With all the additions, by the end of 1942, the hospital had almost doubled in size.

Allentown State Hospital was considered a modern facility that provided the best medical treatments of its time. It was the first state hospital to no longer use seclusion as a treatment—a discontinuation that occurred in 1998. As treatment of mental illness moved to outpatient programs, many mental hospitals were targeted for closure, and Allentown State Hospital announced its closure in 2010. Since then, the building has sat unused and abandoned. In 2019, a bill was passed to demolish the hospital. By the time this book makes it to print, nothing will be left of the hospital but its historic past.

Exploring ASH was an adventure I will never forget. I will not go into detail as to how the adventure came to be, but what I can tell you is that I got to watch the sunrise here a few times with some great friends. We spent hours exploring, venturing down the long connecting corridors along with the massive tunnel system below the building. I can say with confidence this building could have—and should have—been saved.

A view of the administration building from the massive lawn along the oval drive in front of the Allentown State Hospital campus.

The winding staircase in the administration
building was beautiful and made of marble.

The way the light was coming through the windows
as the sun rose created a neat effect.

The courtyards were dense with overgrowth.

This is the balcony overlooking the rotunda entry way of the hospital.

Pictured above is one of the two chapels located in the hospital.

The auditorium was used to host plays, talent shows, and even pageants. It remained elegant even in ruin.

Right: There was a total of forty-three hydrotherapy tubs in the hospital. Patients would sit in these tubs for extended periods of time, in temperatures specifically targeted to suit their conditions.

Below: One of the rooms in the medical building that still had medicine bottles left behind.

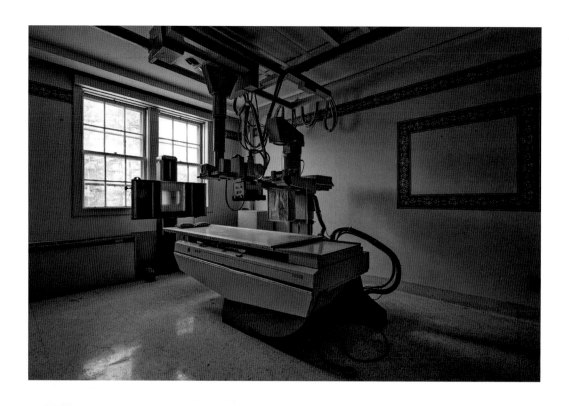

Above: An old x-ray machine remained in the medical building.

Left: The small morgue located in the medical building.

Right: A long connecting hallway.

Below: The infamous pink room was once lined with patient beds. The room was painted pink as it was said that the color was calming for patients.

A more modern bathroom that was located in the admissions building.

A rooftop view of the cupula on top of the administration building.

2

BIRCHWOOD RESORT

B irchwood was said to have been built on an old farm in the 1950s. The property is located in Tannersville, Pennsylvania, on almost 300 acres of land with streams, ponds, and lakes. The resort property is home to many outbuildings, including an indoor bowling alley, a reception center, a lodge, an indoor basketball court, an indoor tennis court, an indoor pool, a ballroom, restaurant, a nightclub, an airplane hangar, and an airstrip.

Back in the 1960s, Birchwood was known as a honeymoon hotspot. The resort had private cottages that were placed alongside the lake. In 1969, the airpark was added to the resort, allowing honeymooners and visitors to fly directly to the resort. The resort offered couples packages that featured mini golf, paddle boats, badminton, bowling, private cabins, and access to the nightclub. An old brochure also advertised gliding over the Poconos and Delaware Water Gap after taking off from the resort's runway. The airpark closed down in 1996, followed by the resort, which shut its doors in 2000.

There is not much written about the old Birchwood Resort prior to the capture of Eric Frein, a gunman who killed a Pennsylvania State trooper in 2014. Frein was found hiding out in the abandoned airplane hangar at Birchwood Pocono Airpark, located on the Birchwood Resort property. The cop who came up to me while I attempted to photograph the property told me that the police found Frein walking naked down the airstrip after a forty-eight-day manhunt.

I wanted so badly to see this property inside and out; however, I did not get very far before the police showed up and requested I leave. Here is what I was able to capture before almost being captured myself.

Shortly after my visit, part of the resort caught fire, damaging some of the buildings.

Words of welcome and of warning.

The Plymouth Cottages along Eagle Lake at Birchwood.

Above left: Across the lake, a small cottage can be seen falling into ruin.

Above right: One of the many cottages on the property.

Furniture still sits on the porch of the registration building. Believe it or not, this building was once red.

Above: There was furniture left behind in almost every room of the cottages.

Left: A shot of the pool deck from the grass below.

Above: A drone shot from 400 feet above of the deck and pool.

Right: Christmas lights strewn across the road. I bet this property was beautiful in its heyday.

3

THE BLUE HORIZON

The Blue Horizon was built in 1865 and was originally three four-story row homes. Around 1912, the building was converted into a Moose Lodge that held events such as cabarets and meetings. An auditorium and a ballroom built by architect Carl Berger was added to the structure in 1916. In the late 1930s, a four-bout boxing event was held at the Moose Lodge, often referred to as "Moose Hall."

In 1960, Jimmy Toppi bought the property after the members of the Moose Lodge moved to another lodge in the area. Jimmy Toppi was inspired by a song called "Beyond the Blue Horizon," which led him to rename the building the Blue Horizon. In 1961, the Blue Horizon held its first boxing match between Chico Corsey of Chester, Pennsylvania, against North Philly's middleweight George Benton. The event was supposed to last ten rounds, but Benton won with a knockout after only three rounds.

The Blue Horizon earned itself the reputation as the best place to host boxing events in Philadelphia, and possibly the entire United States. The venue could hold a capacity of 1,300 people. Between 1961 and 2010, the Blue Horizon saw many boxers begin and end their careers inside its walls.

In 2010, the venue shut its doors due to a license violation. Today, the building sits empty and in disrepair. A current hotel proposal puts the auditorium at risk of being demolished, including demolishing all the buildings, except for the front facade. The Preservation Alliance of Greater Philadelphia successfully lobbied for the Blue Horizon to be included in the Philadelphia Register of Historic Places in 2015, in the hope of saving it from demolition.

My access to this building is a story in itself. I had to call a number that was secretly given out, meet a man in the back alley, and pay him twenty dollars. If you're saying to yourself, "That sounds sketchy," it was. I will never forget being led into the dark by a homeless man who had just taken my money without saying a word to me. I tried to tell myself this was perfectly normal as I stumbled in the dark. When I finally made it to the auditorium and saw the boxing ring, a rush of excitement washed away my fear. The only words the man spoke to me were "thirty minutes," and he left. Within a half hour, he came back to walk me out.

A streetside view of the Blue Horizon.

The boxing ring from the balcony. The decorative woodwork was beautiful. Unfortunately, the seats were removed before I was able to explore this location.

A boxing glove left behind.

I was surprised to find the electric was still working inside the auditorium.

4

CINTRA MANSION

The Cintra mansion is located in New Hope, Pennsylvania. The mansion is four stories high and made of field stone. It was built around 1816 by William Maris, a Philadelphia businessman, who modeled the design after a castle in Lisbon, Portugal. In addition, Maris built a cotton mill and the Delaware House, which is also located in New Hope.

The floor plan of the Cintra mansion includes a rear piazza, a central octagonal entrance with symmetrical flanking wings, and a hipped roof. Also located on the property are two tiny cottages that were once used as an icehouse and a kitchen. The home was later obtained by a woman named Ruth Ely. Ely was rumored to have had a fugitive named Henry Lee as her servant. The last known owner of the mansion was an antique dealer named Joseph Stanley.

After Stanley's death in 2008, the mansion has since fallen into ruin. Today there are plans to turn the almost 205-year-old mansion into apartments. However, not much restoration has been done, and the building still lies empty.

The mansion has a unique layout that is not often seen in the United States.

5

CRIER IN THE COUNTRY

Crier in the Country was a banquet hall, restaurant, and inn located in Glen Mills, Pennsylvania. There are many rumors surrounding this location. It is said that the rear portion of the building dates back to the early 1700s. Research suggests that the original structure was a Victorian mansion and was used as a private residence. The front portion of the building was added in 1861.

As the property exchanged hands, the use of the structure changed as well. In the 1940s, it was used as a retirement home. Then it became a restaurant in the late 1960s, called Deveraux's Fox Crest Inn. An ad for the Deveraux's Fox Crest Inn can be found in the *Delaware County Daily Times* dated March 12, 1970, on page 22 of the paper.

The building remained the inn before eventually becoming Crier in the Country in 1983. Offering fine dining, jazz, and banquet facilities, Crier in the Country stayed in business until it closed in 2007. That same year, an application was submitted, proposing to renovate the property. However, the application was withdrawn after local preservationists fought off the catering company who had proposed a major renovation to the building.

The historic property sat empty until it was demolished in 2017. Located today on the lot of land where the Crier once stood is a senior living facility.

The main entrance of Crier in the Country.

Above left: This exploration was quite a unique one for me. I had heard stories from other explorers of police pointing guns in their faces and people getting caught here frequently. Fortunately, I had better luck. I was able to explore the property thoroughly. I only wish there had been more left inside.

Above right: Vines creeping into the building through broken windows and cracks in the foundation.

Much of what was left inside was in the banquet hall.

Part of the property included a few guest rooms. These can be seen above to the left.

Jacaranda trees growing through cracks of the cement behind the building.

Blooming purple flowers on a jacaranda tree blocks the view. Taken from the window inside the back of the building.

6

DIXIE CUP FACTORY

T he Dixie Cup's story begins in 1907, when Lawrence Luellen came up with the idea for a disposable, individual drinking cup. Luellen then created a one-piece pleated cup, made of a circular blank of paper that was treated with paraffin to hold the folds in place. In 1908, Luellen started the American Water Supply Company of New England with a group of investors.

In an attempt to expand distribution, Luellen and Hugh Moore organized the American Water Supply Company of New York. Luellen and Moore chose to consolidate the operation into one organization in 1910, and so the Individual Drinking Cup Company of New York was incorporated in Maine. Patents for the new company allowed the company to manufacture the cups.

By 1912, the Individual Drinking Cup Company's product was called the Health Kup. After World War I, the Spanish Flu epidemic had created a high demand for paper cups. As competition emerged, Moore changed the name of the product in the hope it would set it apart. In 1919, the Health Kup was changed to the Dixie Cup, named after a New York doll line made by Alfred Schindler's Dixie Doll Company.

A new plant was built in Easton, Pennsylvania, in 1921, and employed seventy-eight workers. The plant was 80,000 square feet and cost about $280,000 to build. On the top of the factory, a giant Dixie Cup was constructed. In 1923, Dixie teamed up with Weed's Ice Cream Company of Allentown and started selling individual servings of ice cream in a Dixie Cup.

In 1955, the giant Dixie Cup was used as a water tower during Hurricane Diane. The Easton plant shut down in 1980 after workers were moved to another location. The plant was sold to investors, who have since had hopes to turn the property into apartments and commercial space; however, due to asbestos and other contaminants, the property currently sits in dereliction.

A unique view of the giant iconic Dixie Cup from a bathroom window.

190 jobs were lost when the plant closed.

Light fixtures falling from the ceiling in the office spaces of the plant.

All the equipment inside the building has been removed.

The floors of the factory are nine inches thick, with solid concrete columns located every ten feet.

Above left: The factory is four stories high and totals 608,000 square feet.

Above right: The giant water tank on top of the factory was painted to resemble a Dixie Cup and can hold up to 40,000 gallons.

7

EMBREEVILLE STATE HOSPITAL

E mbreeville State Hospital was originally the Chester County Almshouse. The Almshouse was built in 1798 to care for the poor, neglected, and insane, though in 1898, the Almshouse moved to a new location. The 225 acres housed sixteen buildings, including a power plant. In 1938, the Commonwealth of Pennsylvania took over the property and it became the Embreeville State Hospital.

Over time, other modern buildings were built to accommodate the increasing mentally ill population who came from Lancaster County and Chester County. The American Psychiatric Association recognized Embreeville as one of the top three model hospitals for mental health care in the country. In 1971, some of the buildings were used as a juvenile detention center.

In 1980, Embreeville no longer operated as a state hospital due to a drop in state hospital census. A portion of the hospital property was utilized for many educational and institutional uses, until the remaining buildings were vacated in 2010. In 2012, the property was purchased by a developer who planned to re-zone the property to build residential homes, along with some commercial zoning. The property was zoned for institutional and mixed-use at the time the proposal was submitted. After almost seven years of hearings and appeals, the redevelopment company and the West Bradford Township came to an agreement; however, as a settlement was attempting to be reached, these buildings still sat abandoned and left to the elements. In February 2020, the developer began demolition of the buildings.

The stillness and quiet on the campus was an eerie experience.

A few of the buildings had rooms with round areas. Many of them were empty, giving no clues as to their use.

Books and office equipment were left on a desk in one of the administrative offices.

The swimming pool was heavily covered in graffiti and appeared to be just a few feet deep.

Every step down the hallways resulted in a crunching sound as the tiles broke beneath my feet.

A wheelchair sitting in a room of the Woodview building.

Furniture left behind in what appears to be a patient room.

The gymnasium floor was warped from water damage.

The signs above the door read "Pennsylvania Clinical Schools."

8

IREM TEMPLE

Construction of the Irem Temple began in 1907 and was completed in 1908. Located in Wilkes-Barre, Pennsylvania, the temple has a large stained-glass dome and four towering minarets, which separate it from other Irem Shriners auditoriums. In 1931, a sloped floor, auditorium seating, and a stage replaced the original flat-floor auditorium design. For most of the twentieth century, the temple was used for ritual and social events, for both the Irem Shriners and the Wilkes-Barre community. The once-filled venue became vacant when it closed in the 1990s.

In 2005, the structure was purchased by the Greater Wilkes-Barre Chamber of Commerce with the goal to preserve and renew the building. In 2008, critical roof repairs were done. These repairs ultimately saved the building from a demolition crew. Nonetheless, the financial crisis of 2008 was devasting to the restoration of the building, and the Chamber of Commerce had to discontinue their efforts. In 2019, the Irem Temple Restoration Project (ITRP) obtained the property and is working towards restoration of the temple. It is their hope to have it host large concerts, weddings, banquets, and other events.

Above: The temple has such a unique shape to it.

Right: The front door of the Irem Temple is designed lavishly in the Moorish Revival style.

Above: A couch left behind in one of the rooms that adjoined the main auditorium.

Left: Taken from the projector room above the auditorium, you can see the stage, dome, and seating below.

The auditorium once had red carpeting. It has since been removed, exposing the hardwood floors.

Twin staircases on either side of the main entrance lead to the second floor as well as the basement.

Above: Paint chips from the ceiling litter the auditorium chairs.

Left: On the stage lay a dead hawk near what appears to be some kind of filing cabinet.

An old, tattered horse costume left behind.

Light fixtures (with the lightbulbs intact) strung across the ceiling above. These lights were once used to illuminate the massive dome.

9

J. W. COOPER SCHOOL

Located in Pennsylvania's coal county is the J. W. Cooper School, which was originally named the Shenandoah High School. The name was later changed in honor of Jonathan W. Cooper, who was superintendent of Shenandoah's schools from 1897 to 1927. The school was designed by architect Austin J. Reilly.

Construction began in 1917 and finished in 1918. But before the school was able to open, it was used as a hospital and morgue during the Spanish influenza. In 1919, the school officially began operating as a school, serving as a high school from 1919 to 1968. From 1968 to 1986, it served as an elementary school.

The building measures 45,000 square feet and is two stories high on the front elevation and four stories on the rear elevation. The structure, designed in the classic revival style, is built of sandstone and brick. The school features an auditorium with a skylight, a gymnasium with an elevated jogging track, and an indoor swimming pool. The school was originally attached to an older building that contained a library with additional classrooms; however, that building was demolished in the late 1980s. The auditorium can accommodate 800 people with two levels of seating and features atrium windows. A past owner removed the original brass railing and stained-glass windows.

The gymnasium was located on the first floor while the second floor housed the pool, the track, multiple classrooms, and locker rooms. The third floor contains classrooms, bathrooms, the auditorium stage, and first-level seating as well as an office. The auditorium balcony is located on the fourth floor along with more classrooms and a nurse's office.

The school closed in the early 1990s. It sat unused for nearly nineteen years before it was purchased by a local jewelry-store owner, who hopes to turn the school into a community center.

The location and design of the school made it challenging to get a good shot.

The front of the building has two entrances labeled "Boys" and "Girls," as was typical of the period in which it operated.

The school's swimming pool is the oldest swimming pool located inside of a school in the state of Pennsylvania.

There was originally a spiral staircase located in the gymnasium that allowed people to access the track from the first floor, but it was removed and sold.

The ceiling of the auditorium was originally illuminated by a large skylight.

Ceiling plaster rests on a pile of broken chairs in the auditorium.

Left: Most of the classrooms were empty, except for a few that still contained a few chairs with desks.

Below: Weeds growing out of the floor of an old classroom.

10

LIVINGSTON LANE

It has been nearly impossible to find information about this location. What little I could unearth suggests it was the Lochiel Farm. The lane currently sits abandoned, with three houses located along the overgrown road.

Possibly Lochiel Farm.

The road was lined with thousands of small trees, making it almost impossible to see the houses.

The largest of the houses along the road was the most damaged.

Right: The last house on the lane was my favorite.

Below: This property had two entrances, one of which with a large tree trunk strewn across the road.

NO TRESPASSING PRIVATE DRIVEWAY

11

LYNNEWOOD HALL

Lynnewood Hall was designed by Horace Trumbauer, a famed Philadelphia architect. The 110-room mansion was built in 1898 for streetcar tycoon, Peter Arrell Browne (P. A. B.) Widener. It is considered one of the finest homes in the Philadelphia area.

P. A. B. Widener was an art collector, philanthropist, and businessman. Widener also partook in the organization of the American Tobacco Company and the United States Steel Corporation. Lynnewood Hall is a two-story, seventeen-bay Classical Revival mansion constructed from limestone and designed in a T-shape. The main entrance leads into a two-story grand hall. The grand hall has a black-and-white checkered marble floor and a coffered ceiling with a yellow stained-glass window in the center. The cross arm of the "T" consists of immense wings that extend east and west from the grand hall. The east wing on the first floor contains a reception hall, a gallery, and a ballroom.

The first-floor west wing contains a dining room, a smoking room, and a pantry. The second-story east wing was used for private living and contains mostly bedrooms. The east wing was also where Widener's oldest son, George, and his family lived. The west wing on the second floor contains the living quarters of the master, along with those of his son Joseph and Joseph's family. The north wing housed the library, offices, and servant areas on the first floor. The second floor included a tearoom, an art gallery, and guest rooms. There was an indoor swimming pool, a squash court, and another art gallery, known as the Van Dyck Gallery, located in the rear addition of the north wing. The grounds of the mansion were landscaped by a French architect, Jacques Greber, who decorated the grounds with fountains, roses, and parterre gardens.

Lynnewood was once self-sustaining. What is now the apartment complex Lynnewood Gardens, located on the south side of Asbourne Road (originally Cheltenham Ave), sat a 117-acre farm. The farm had stock barns, horse stables, greenhouses, chicken houses, and a half-mile racetrack with a polo field in the middle. In addition to the farm, the estate had its own power plant, carpentry shop, bakery, laundry facility, and water pumps. At any given time, there were thirty-seven full-time servants on staff.

In 1912, Widener's son, George, along with George's wife and their son, Harry, perished in the sinking of the RMS *Titanic*. Widener had been an investor in the *Titanic* and his family was traveling home from a trip to Europe. Then, in 1916, P. A. B Widener passed away inside the home. Widener's son Joseph inherited the home and, in the 1920s, opened Lynnewood Hall to the public. The opening of the private gallery lent to Lynnewood's art collection gaining international recognition. The Widener family remained in Lynnewood until 1941, and Joseph passed away in 1943.

The property sat unclaimed by Joseph's children, vacant and left to be looked after by the caretaker. A developer purchased the home in 1948, but nothing was done to the property, and it fell into disrepair. In 1952, the mansion was purchased by Faith Theological Seminary, who used the mansion as a chapel, school, and living space. Much of the mansion was therefore altered. The fountains were sold in 1989, and in 1993, the Faith Theological Seminary attempted to sell architectural components of the mansion. Thankfully, the sale was halted. In 1996, Richard S. Yoon purchased the mansion at a sheriff's sale. Yoon's plan was to turn the mansion into part of his church, the First Korean Church of New York. Due to the cost of the property and the upkeep, the mansion was listed for sale in 2014 for $20 million dollars. No sale was made, and in 2017, the property was relisted again at $17 million.

Above: The mansion stretches 365 feet from east to west and sits on 33.85 acres of gated land.

Left: The green carpeted staircase in the grand hall is gorgeous and one of a kind. Surrounded by composite pilasters that are flanked by large stone arches, the grand staircase is decorated with iron rails. The staircase divides to winding stairs that lead to the second-floor balcony.

This was one of my favorite rooms in the mansion. I found it peculiar that the mirror was shattered, but there was no glass on the floor and old newspapers were still inside the fireplace.

The chapel, once used as the ballroom, measures 2,550 square feet with walnut-paneled walls. The columns and filigree plaster are decorated in gold leaf, and the ceiling displays angelic figures with floral-motif molding accented in gold leaf.

An empty picture frame hangs on the wall of a forgotten guest room.

This mother-of-pearl-like elongated dome is centered in the ceiling above what was once the tearoom.

This classroom located in the east wing was once used as a gallery. Though this room has been altered, it still features a beautiful polychrome wood-beamed ceiling.

The view from the east wing, looking down towards the grand hall.

A beautiful reception room, located on the first floor of the mansion, is decorated with wood paneling and gold-leaf accents.

Above left: The second floor of the mansion consists of many rooms with passages that take you room to room.

Above right: Furniture left behind in one of the guest rooms.

An elaborate iron rail decorates the staircase and the second-story balcony that overlooks the grand hall.

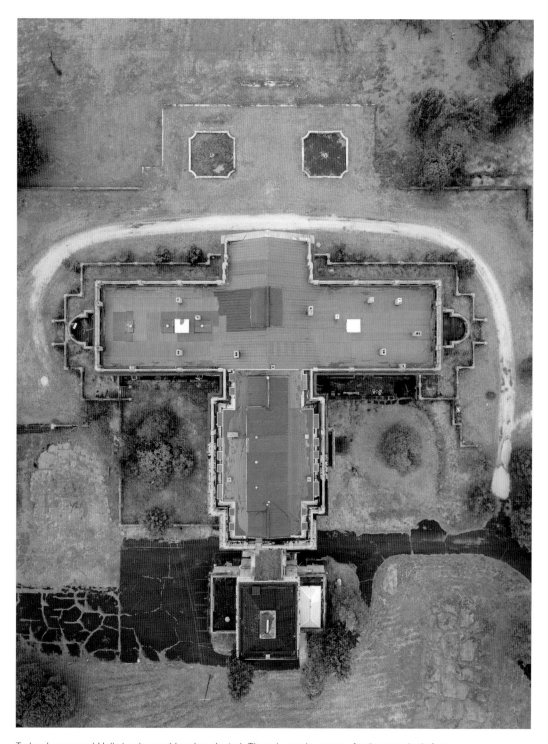

Today, Lynnewood Hall stands unsold and neglected. There is much concern for the mansion's future.

12

McDERMITT CONCRETE

McDermitt was a concrete contractor located in Gettysburg, Pennsylvania. After extensive research, I was able to find out that the concrete and asphalt plant went up for bankruptcy. Located on the property were two houses, a main control tower, an asphalt plant, a flat conveyor to silo, a diesel-powered heating tank, and numerous other machineries.

The main building on the property was locked, so I was unable to explore the inside.

In one of the rooms there was
a pile of what appeared to be
decals or stickers.

Every door was left open,
except for the main building.

A fire extinguisher still hanging from a light pole near the fueling station.

Looking up an old conveyor belt.

Water hoses hang from a derelict conveyor system.

This home was located at the entrance of the property. Today, this is the only building left.

13

NAZARETH SPEEDWAY

Nazareth Speedway was built in 1910 in Lehigh Valley, Pennsylvania. It was originally a dirt tri-oval layout. In 1966, the motor-racing circuit was renovated and reopened as the Nazareth National Speedway. The track remained open until it closed in 1984. Roger Penske then purchased the track in 1987. The tri-oval track was paved and reopened in 1987 as the Pennsylvania International Raceway. In 1993, the track was renamed Nazareth Speedway, then in 1997, improvements were made to the track, including a new retaining wall, grandstands, and catch fence.

Nazareth Speedway hosted many events such as the Busch Series and the Indy Racing League races. The track saw much success; however, it closed in 2004 after a new owner took over the facility. In 2007, the grandstand and pedestrian bridge were removed. Although the land was purchased in 2015 by Raceway Properties, LLC, there are no plans to return racing to the track. Part of the property's sale included a clause that banned racing on the property due to how close the track is located to the Pocono Raceway.

On my visit to the track sixteen years after its closing, I was happy to find there were still several concessions stands, souvenir shops, and a restroom facility. The black-and-white checkers of the victory lane were also still visible on the pavement.

Above: The tunnel was used as an entrance and exit to the infield.

Left: A view of the tunnel leading to the infield.

Right: Winner's circle.

Below left: A view from the pit road of the announcers building.

Below right: Weeds storm the cracks of the concession area.

14

PENNHURST STATE SCHOOL AND HOSPITAL

Pennhurst, originally known as the Eastern Pennsylvania Institution for the Feeble Minded and Epileptic, opened its doors in 1908. The institution sits on 1,400 acres of land located in both Montgomery County and Chester County. The state-funded school and hospital consists of more than thirty buildings, including a farm, a morgue, a barber shop, a fire house, and even its own power plant. The institution was committed to the study, care, education, and employment training of intellectually disabled girls and boys who had parents that resided in the eastern half of the state of Pennsylvania.

Pennhurst offered schooling from kindergarten to seventh grade. The completion of the school's elementary program allowed girls to transfer to home economic development and the boys to attend manual training shops. Upon completion of manual training shops, the boys could paint and refinish furniture, among many other skills. When the girls completed home economics, they were able to press, mend, and sew, as well as serve meals. It was believed that learning these skills gave patients a sense of accomplishment and improved development of their social skills. At Pennhurst, music, religious services, physical recreation, and physical education were also available to the patients, with each activity supervised by various staff.

Pennhurst changed from a model institution that was recognized by the American Hospital Association to being referred to as "the shame of Pennsylvania." In 1968, Channel 10 news broadcasted a five-episode exposé by Bill Baldini. Baldini's *Suffer the Little Children* series revealed the inhumane conditions at Pennhurst State School and Hospital. During the eight decades that Pennhurst was in operation, it was "home" to around 10,600 adults and children with cognitive disabilities. The footage in Baldini's report shows scenes of patients strapped to beds, lying on the cold floor, or contained in cribs. Other footage shows patients sitting on the floor, rocking themselves, and others wandering around half-naked in overcrowded rooms. The sounds heard through the microphone were haunting.

At the time of the documentary, Pennhurst housed 2,791 patients while the hospital had a maximum capacity of 1,984 patients. The number of staff employed at this time was only 800, and by the late 1960s, only a few hundred patients were in any kind of recreational program. The buildings were deteriorating to the point of being unsafe, and no longer met state requirements for operation.

After the documentary aired, the state school and hospital became the center of a human-rights movement that eventually revolutionized America's approach to mental healthcare. In 1987, due to inadequate staffing, overcrowding, lack of funds, years of abuse and neglect allegations, and the groundbreaking case of *Halderman v. Pennhurst State School and Hospital*, Pennhurst closed its doors for good.

The property sat abandoned for twenty years, until it was purchased by Richard Chakejian, who turned a portion of the property into a haunted attraction. Today, much of Pennhurst has either been demolished or lies in ruins.

Pennhurst will forever be one of my favorite explores. The property is massive and holds such a heavy history. It is sad to see it slowly disappearing.

Peeking out the window of the Mayflower building, you can see the playground where the children once played.

Above: Many patients were unable to walk, talk, or dress themselves due to severe understaffing.

Left: You can still see the name "Pennhurst" painted above the entryway of the administration building.

Above left: A broken chair leans against a wall in one of the patient rooms.

Above right: The slide on the playground is rusty and warped. From this view of Pennhurst, it looks like you could slide down from the roof.

Right: Old cafeteria trays and dishes piled up in a room in the Mayflower building.

A Raggedy Ann doll left behind in one of the patient rooms.

A bed and walker left behind in the patient sleeping areas.

A view of Vincennes Hall.

Doctor's House. Now demolished.

15

POCONO'S RESORT

The Pocono Mountains were once a destination for newlyweds and families vacationing. For many of us, when we think of honeymoon resorts, we think of heart shaped tubs and private cottages. Today, the Poconos are filled with abandoned resorts.

One resort in particular remained mostly untouched, unlike neighboring resorts that have been burned, vandalized, or demolished. Due to the condition of the resort, it was purchased and repurposed.

One of the many villas that were on the property.

A heart shaped pool in one of the guest rooms.

A champagne tower located in a villa guest room. These could hold up to eight people but were aimed more toward couples.

16

SCRANTON LACE COMPANY

Scranton Lace Company, originally named the Scranton Lace Curtain Manufacturing Company, was established in 1890 by the Scranton Board of Trade. The company was incorporated in 1897, though it was not until 1916 that the name was changed to Scranton Lace Company. The company was located on Meylert Avenue in Scranton, Pennsylvania. Between the years of 1916 and 2002, Scranton Lace Company was the first, largest, and leading known producer of Nottingham lace in the United States. Among the products the company made were napkins, tablecloths, shower curtains, valences, and more. In the 1940s during World War II, the company worked with Sweeny Bros and Victory Parachutes, Inc. to manufacture camouflage netting and parachutes. At one point, Scranton Lace Company had 1,600 employees. The large property consisted of thirty-four buildings that totaled over 600,000 square feet.

The Scranton Lace Factory takes up about five city blocks. Its buildings included a bowling alley, a theater, a gymnasium, a barber shop, and an infirmary. Risky investments in the 1950s led the company into a financial spiral that ultimately led to its closure in 2002. The property then sat empty with hopes of redevelopment. Even though the factory was added to the National Register of Historic Places in 2012, demolition began on the property in 2018.

Scranton Lace Factory was such an awesome place to see. I conquered my fear of heights here by climbing the clock tower. This place was huge, so it was impossible to explore all of it in one day. In total, I returned three times, and each time, I saw something new. I have never climbed so many stairs in my life.

The factory shut down and closed its doors in the middle of the day. Lace can be seen dangling from the loom, frozen in time.

Taken from one of the skyway bridges, the buildings appear to go on forever.

Thread spills out of a bin surrounded by old lace patterns.

All the shipping boxes had the Scranton Lace Co. logo printed on the sides.

Above left: A skein of yarn sits atop the basketball hoop.

Above right: A broken window in the factory offered a unique view.

Right: A warped hallway in the office area of the factory.

Lace pours out of a canvas basket truck.

Only one of the looms remained in the factory.

A room was filled with canvas basket trucks used for material handling.

The clock tower has a Meneely cast-iron bell and is a city landmark.

17

SNYDER'S MILL

Along the Perkiomen Creek sits Snyder's Mill. The mill is a four-story structure with five dormer windows and a hip roof. The first floor is made of fieldstone, with the upper stories made of bricks.

Built in 1891, the mill produced flour and cattle feed. While all the equipment has been removed, the property is still home to the master house and mill building. The master house is a three-story brick Victorian manor home. The home has sat abandoned for many, many years. Today, it is currently for sale, waiting to be saved.

The master house sits back from the road.

The creek runs below the mill and leads to frequent flooding.

18

THIRD PRESBYTERIAN CHURCH

The Third Presbyterian Church, located in Chester, Pennsylvania, was built in 1895 and held its first service in May of 1896. This Gothic-style church was designed by architect Isaac Pursell. Pursell designed the cathedral much like a ship, framing it with iron turnbuckles along with a separate outer wooden frame that was decorated with terracotta tiles. The Celadon Tile Company of Alfred, New York, manufactured and shipped the tiles to Chester by rail for over 200 miles.

While the outside of the church is reminiscent of the Renaissance Era, the inside was very American. An overhead glass window within the rotunda provided an abundance natural lighting. There was a wall of windows that could be raised like a garage door that allowed the sanctuary and rotunda to become one big open space. The church had classrooms, deep windowsills that allowed floral displays, a wall of glass-covered bookcases, and a ladies' parlor with a fireplace. The church shut its doors in 1986 when the congregation could no longer keep the church. The Chester Eastside Ministries owned the building until 2013 but were unable to keep maintaining the building. The Chester Historic Preservation Committee (CHPC) purchased the building in 2015, after it sat empty for three years. CHPC had hopes to restore the building to its former glory and turn it into a center for the performing arts and a venue for weddings and other events.

Tragedy struck on May 28, 2020, when a fire broke out around 2:30 in the morning. For several hours, firefighters fought to put out the five-alarm fire. There were no active electrical components inside the church, and the church did not have electricity or running water. The fire remains under suspicion. Where this massive, one-of-a-kind church stood is now only a shell of what it once was.

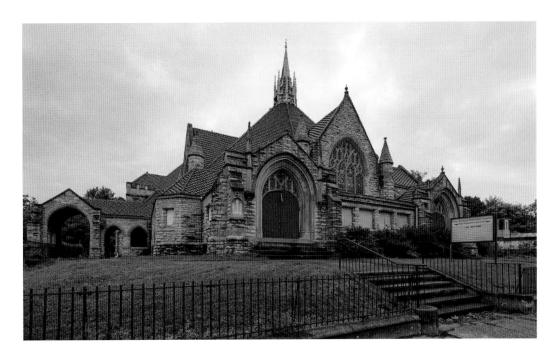

Above: The church was massive and unique in many ways.

Right: A view of the stage from the pews.

Light bursts through the stained glass.

The library still stocked with books.

After I heard about the fire, I was on my way to photograph a mansion nearby, so I went out to see it for myself. Luckily for me, a man was there who was hired to put up the fence to keep people out. He let me onto the property to photograph the aftermath.

19

VOLKSWAGEN GRAVEYARD

Deep in the woods sit dozens of abandoned Volkswagen Beetles, Campervans, Buses, Golfs, and even Karmann Ghias. What was once a parts warehouse and a junkyard specializing in Volkswagens has now become a graveyard for them. There is not much information about why the business closed or the fate of the cars.

Volkswagen buses lined the main drive that leads to the warehouse on the property.

Left: Bumpers rest on top of an Mk1 Rabbit.

Below: There were a few Volkswagen Type 4s among the Beetles.

Next to the warehouse was a mix of Volkswagen cars, including Rabbits, a Beetle, a Bus, and a Jetta.

One side of the property was a maze of Beetles in every direction.

20

YORK PRISON

In 1855, a castle-like stone-wall prison was built on Chestnut Street in York, Pennsylvania. York Prison, as it was called, was built to house Civil War prisoners. The original stone-wall prison was demolished and replaced with a five-story, 30,000-square-foot brick multi-story cellblock prison in 1906. Architect B. F. Willis designed the prison, along with trap-door-style gallows where hangings took place. The prison had a total of eighty-two cells. In the 1950s, rumors circulated that people in the prison were being placed in padded cells to save on space, there was racial segregation during the night hours, and that the only meat served for two weeks was venison, sourced from roadkill brought back by police.

In 1979, the prison closed its doors and the property sat abandoned for nearly two decades. Although the prisoners are gone, the prison is filled with piles of peeling paint, poison ivy, and old furniture. In 1982, John and Joyce Gearhart purchased the prison, wanting to turn the building into a jail-themed restaurant (their idea was to have different dining options on each floor). Then, in 2003, the York Street Community Center considered purchasing the prison to use as a parking lot. In 2007, the Gearharts put up the prison for sale for $3.9 million. They handed out posters that read: "Wanted: $25,000 reward for the capture of a buyer for the Old York County Prison."

Ideas were tossed around for years of what would happen with the old prison: a baseball stadium, loft apartments, and another restaurant idea. There was even talk of making the prison a haunted attraction. But in 2014, York's Redevelopment Authority took possession of the Old York County Prison and surrounding property by reason of eminent domain, stating that the property was blighted (dilapidated). The court ruled that the fair-market value of the prison was $292,000; however, this is not the amount they offered the Gearharts. Instead, the York Redevelopment Authority argued that it would cost them close to $230,000 to remove lead paint and asbestos from the building. The Gearharts appealed the court's decision of $65,000 compensation of the property, arguing that the property was purchased for $3.9 million. After almost five years of appeals, the court determined that at the time the York Redevelopment Authority seized the land, it was worth $1.2 million at fair-market value price, and so the court ordered the city to pay the Gearharts. In 2018, the York Development Authority found a way to get out of the $1.2-million payment by entering a settlement with a tech company, United Fiber and Data.

Most recently, the abandoned prison has been rumored to be turned into a hub in United Fiber and Data's 400-mile fiber-optic network. But today, the prison sits empty, and no work has begun.

Taken from across the street, you can see how immense the structure is.

"York County Prison" painted above the main entrance. Today, this entrance is plastered over by concrete and the sign is no longer visible.

Paint chips off the walls of an eerie empty cell block.

A collapsed table in one of the cell blocks.

An empty cell with rusty bunks and a pillowcase covered with paint chips.

It appears as if some of the bars have been cut out of this cell block.

Every window on the prison was secured with iron bars that hold strong, even today.

This prison gave me nightmares shortly after visiting. The only way into the prison was this small hole that appeared to have been chiseled out by an unknown person. Outside of the hole was a suitcase that was filled with clean clothes and hats. I could only assume that this person left the suitcase outside because they could not fit it through the hole. It is important I point out that this hole was the only way in and out of the abandoned prison, as all the windows had bars and the front door was chained. I remember being on edge the entire time and feeling I just wanted to get out of there.